Looking at ANIMALS

INVADER

kennel

dog

dog

dog

bowl

cat

cat basket

cat

cat

bowl

horse and rider

stable

pony

calf

cow

sheep

lamb

chicken

chick

chicken coop

cockerel

pig

piglet

rabbit

baby rabbits

drake

duck

ducklings

young
swan
swan
cygnets

elephant

baby
elephant

bear

bear cub

donkey

baby donkey

kid

goat

butterfly

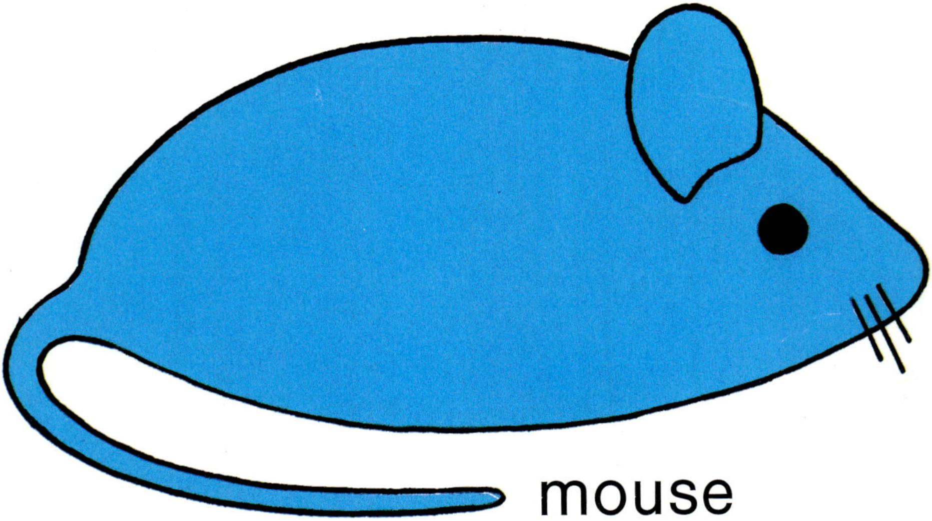

mouse

fish

owl

duck

tortoise

stork
frog

lion
lion cub

panda

tiger

giraffe

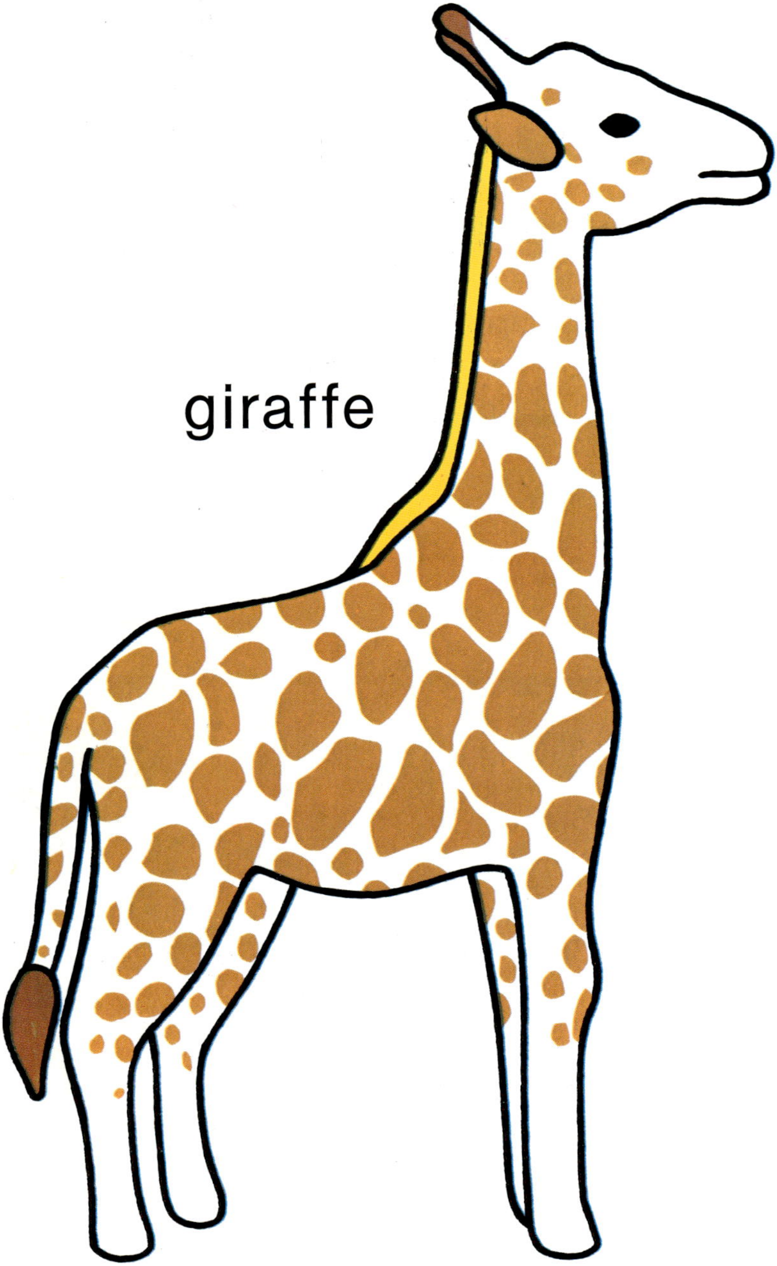

camel

deer
fawn

zebra

fox

guinea pig

hedgehog

snake

parrot

caterpillar

seal

whale

kangaroo